Where Can Spike Sleep?

by Catherine Casey
illustrated by Ayesha L. Rubio

OXFORD
UNIVERSITY PRESS

Spike was curled up in a bed of leaves. He had settled in a bush for the winter. Hazel snoozed on a branch higher up.

Suddenly, Spike was woken up by a loud noise.
The ground shook and rumbled.

“Hazel, how can you sleep?” Spike complained.

“Leave me to snooze,” grumbled Hazel.

“Come on, let’s investigate,” replied Spike.

Spike poked his head out from the bush. He heard deafening diggers and lots of trucks. Spike could smell fresh soil.

"What is it?" asked Hazel.

"It is a construction site. There are humans in hard hats and yellow jackets. They are driving noisy diggers and trucks," replied Spike.

“That sounds awful!” said Hazel.

“We cannot stay here! We must find another place to sleep,” Spike cried.

Spike began to shuffle off.

“Spike, listen. The noise is stopping. I think they are leaving,” suggested Hazel.

“They will come back in the morning. Humans don’t like the dark,” said Spike.

As the sun started to set, Spike trundled off.
He was determined to find another place to settle.
Hazel followed her friend.

The next morning, Spike found a spot under a hedge. He made a new nest. Spike and Hazel drifted off to sleep. It was not long before the sun came up.

Cars began to whizz past. Loud horns beeped all day long. Spike and Hazel's hedge was by a main road.

“Oh dear, I cannot stay here,” complained Spike. “Come on, Hazel, let’s go!” he begged.

“I was sleeping,” moaned Hazel.

Before Hazel had time to think, Spike had left. He was crossing the risky road by himself. A fast car was zooming along.

"Stop!" yelled Hazel.

Spike stepped back just in time.

"You cannot cross that road," squeaked Hazel.

"We will have to go this way, then," announced Spike.

Spike shuffled off along the pavement with Hazel. They came to a huge, long brick wall. Spike could not climb like Hazel.

They finally arrived at a park. Spike stepped onto a crinkly packet.

“This park is full of rubbish!” Spike complained.

Spike was right. The park was covered with litter.

“Oh, I am stuck,” squealed Hazel suddenly.

Hazel looked down at her feet. One foot was tangled in a piece of plastic.

Spike slowly nibbled her free.

“I will get my spines stuck if we stay here,” said Spike.

“This place is shocking!” said Hazel sadly.

Spike and Hazel trudged on again. They approached a huge fence made from wood.

“This feels hopeless,” sighed Hazel, looking up at the fence.

Just then they found a little hole in the fence. Spike shuffled into the hole and Hazel followed.

On the other side was a quiet garden. There was a dish of fresh water waiting for them. Spike and Hazel had a long, cool drink.

Then they found a pile of logs. There was also a compost heap. They discovered plenty of bugs and berries to eat.

Best of all, there was a hedgehog house. It was a little wooden hut with leaves and moss in it. Spike and Hazel curled up inside. They finally went to sleep.

Make a Hedgehog House

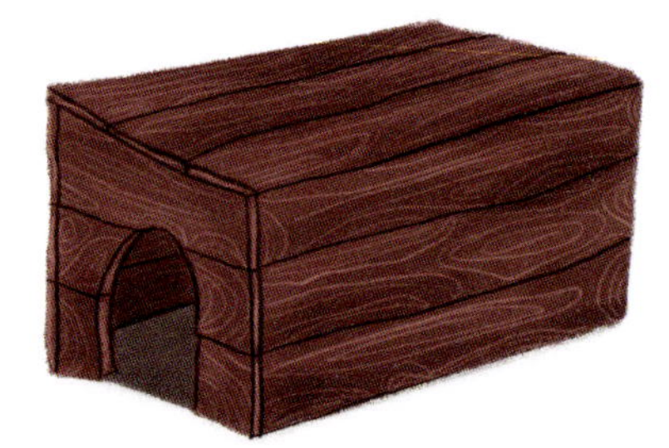

Step 1: Find a quiet, shady spot outside.

Step 2: Place a wooden crate upside down. Ask an adult to cut a hole.

Step 3: Make an entrance with small logs.

Step 4: Make a bed using dry leaves and moss.

Step 5: Cover the house with twigs and leaves.

Encourage students to read through the instructions.
If appropriate, have a go making a hedgehog house together.